Meeting the Needs of Your Dog

Daniel Shaw

Dog Dedication
www.dogdedication.org

ACKNOWLEDGEMENTS

I first began studying canine behaviour after being introduced to the topic by our dog's behaviourist and Natural Animal Centre graduate Boo Blackhurst. Much of what I have learnt is thanks to her encyclopaedic knowledge of dog behaviour that made such a difference to our own dog Misty. I am also grateful to Heather and Ross Simpson, founders of the Natural Animal Centre for all the work they have done for animal welfare and the excellent animal behaviour qualifications they offer. Their canine behaviour course provided me with an excellent introduction to the complex world of dog behaviour, providing a unique physiological understanding of behaviour.

I would also like to thank my own dog, Misty, who I have learnt so much from, and for always reminding me of how much more there is to learn. And my wonderful cats, Alfie and Tiger, for proving to me that it's not just dogs that can be trained.

CONTENTS

Introduction

When I adopted my first dog, I knew very little about dog ownership, and less still about dog behaviour. Of course, I knew she would need to be fed, walked and maybe trained but other than that I just expected her to get on with things. However, Misty turned out to be a far more complicated dog than I ever imagined. Our first discovery was that she was deaf, and we later found out she suffers from partial seizures. On top of this, she is extremely anxious around new people and places and if she becomes stressed will obsessively chase shadows around the house and the garden.

We quickly learnt that Misty had an extremely heightened response to any minor changes in her environment, and that if we set up things up well her stress could greatly be reduced. While this was a challenge, it also provided valuable insight into the needs of dogs. If any of Misty's needs were not met, whether she was hungry, bored, feeling unsafe, tired, under stimulated or over stimulated you would always know.

It was then that Misty's behaviourist introduced me to the Natural Animal Centre's Hierarchy of Needs, developed by Heather and Ross Simpson. It serves as a guideline of the different behavioural needs in dogs and how to meet them. It functions similarly to Maslow's Hierarchy of Needs in humans; which states that for motivation to occur at the next level, each previous need has to be met.

It became apparent to me that meeting the needs of a dog was more complicated than I ever could have imagined. Dogs have adapted to living with humans, which means they live in a very different environment to how they would naturally. As a result of domestication, it is much harder for them to practice natural behaviours that are important to their welfare. While in most dogs, stress is unlikely to cause the level of response that it does for Misty it is important to remember dogs can still experience stress if their needs are not being met. This book explores the steps we can take to help meet the behavioural needs of our canine companions, while also covering some useful training concepts that will help keep training stress free for both you and your dog.

Throughout the book, I refer to all dogs as she. This primarily stems from the fact Misty is a girl, and because she is such a complex case, I am used to writing about her.

Since qualifying as a canine behaviour consultant with the Natural Animal Centre, I have begun working in and around the Kent area in the South East of England. I am now a full member of the Pet Professional Guild and a supporting member of the International Association of Animal Behaviour Consultants. If you are looking for support with your dog (or cat), please do not hesitate to contact me. My business name is Dog Dedication, and you will be able to find more information about my rates and services at: www.dogdedication.org

THE NAC HIERARCHY OF NEEDS IN DOGS

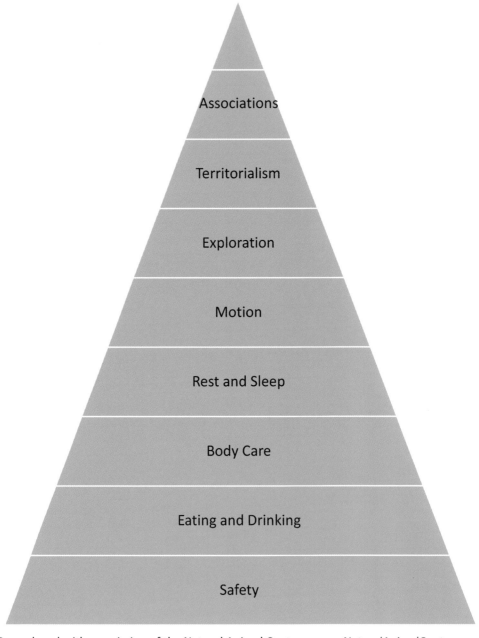

Associations

Territorialism

Exploration

Motion

Rest and Sleep

Body Care

Eating and Drinking

Safety

Reproduced with permission of the Natural Animal Centre - www.NaturalAnimalCentre.com

Chapter 1 - Safety

A sense of safety serves as a base need for many animals. Without this it is a struggle for any of the dog's other needs to be adequately met. One good example of this is fireworks. Many dogs are afraid of the loud banging sounds of fireworks, and often can be found hiding. It is very unlikely you will see a dog in this state eating, resting or playing. This is because their initial need for safety is not being met.

So, what do we mean by a sense of safety? Well, amongst many other things, it can include:

- Feeling safe around other dogs
- Feeling safe around other humans (or any other animal)
- Feeling safe while eating and drinking
- Feeling safe while on the lead
- Feeling safe when out on a walk
- Feeling safe when their owner is away

In this section we will look at how to create this sense of safety, and the first step towards this is being able to recognise when a dog is feeling scared and knowing how to respond. When a dog is fearful, she generally will have one of four potential responses, known as the "four F's", which aim to increase the distance between the threat and themselves:

1. FIGHT

The first of the options is fight. At a high level dogs may display defensive aggression such as lunging, barking or attempting to bite the perceived threat. At this point, it is fairly obvious that the dog is fearful. However, in the initial stages the signs can be subtler, such as a light growl or curled lip, therefore it is very important to be attentive to your dog when out walking and even around the home. If you see your dog becoming fearful, take them out of the situation before it escalates. Many traditional trainers recommend making the dog "face their fears" at this point. However, the danger of this is that the dog will ultimately become more fearful of the threatening object or animal, as she will associate them with a scary experience. It also risks the dog redirecting the fear aggression towards her owner.

The dog on the left has ears tucked back and the dog on the right's pupils are dilated. Both dogs are showing low level signs of fear.

2. FLIGHT

The second option the dog has is flight, to run away from the threat. This is another common method amongst animals, as it reduces the risk of physical injury; something that neither parties really want. However, in the case of our domestic dogs, flight is often difficult to achieve, as dogs spend a lot of the times in the confines of a house or on the lead, leading many dogs to fight instead. Hence why so many dogs are known as "leash reactive", meaning they react fearfully towards other dogs when they are on the lead. To help resolve this, we can create safe spaces for the dog around the house, where she knows she will not be disturbed. Similarly, on walks, if you notice your dog displaying subtle signs of stress, such as ears back, yawning or head bowing, at the approach of another human or dog, you can simply cross the road, or walk in a different direction.

3. FREEZE

When presented with a threat, you may also observe your dog freezing, staying entirely still and motionless. This gives the animal time to evaluate the situation and makes them less likely to be spotted by a potential aggressor as many animals including dogs, have vision best designed to detect motion.

4. FIDDLE ABOUT

The final response is the most difficult to detect, as it can look very much like the dog is behaving normally, but in fact these are specialised behaviours designed to pacify a threat. These behaviours are by far the most common choice when the animal is faced with a non-serious threat. Fiddle about behaviours fall into two categories: **appeasement** and **displacement** behaviours. Appeasement is submissive behaviour designed to pacify the aggressor. This can include things such as lying down, rolling over or averting gaze.

The dog is lying down in an appeasing, pacifying gesture.

Displacement behaviours are normal behaviours displayed in an inappropriate context such as yawning, sniffing the ground, scratching or lip licking. It is really important we are aware and attentive to these behaviours in our dogs to avoid conflicts escalating. If a dog has reached the point of displaying these signals, they are most likely already acting with caution and therefore more likely to react, so it is best to remove them from the situation, at least until they are feeling calmer and more able to cope.

This dog is indicating that he is mildly uncomfortable through a yawn.

THE FOUR "FS"

Appeasement, displacement, freezes and mild fight or flight responses all indicate a dog is uncomfortable and should be removed from the situation. These lower level strategies are all extremely useful communication tools for our dogs. If they are ignored, or punished, the dog may learn that there is no point in using these strategies as they are never successful. This is one reason why we sometimes end up with dogs that go straight into high level responses such as growling, lunging or biting.

It is also really important for dog owners to be aware of and respond to these signals for the safety of both the dog, and others. For example, if a dog bites a child, it may seem shocking and unprovoked, however it is likely that the dog has already displayed subtle signs she is uncomfortable before this, such as pulling her ears back or turning her head away and they have gone unnoticed.

OTHER STEPS CAN WE TAKE TO HELP OUR DOGS FEEL SAFE

As well as knowing their individual limits, we can also take positive steps to make our dogs' feel safer and make life seem less confusing and uncertain.

POSITIVE REINFORCEMENT BASED TRAINING

Positive reinforcement based training is an excellent way to teach your dog to do new things, build a relationship between you and your dog and enrich your dogs' life. As well as it being a kinder way to teach, the advantages of reward-based training are very practical:

- Rate of Learning is improved – Dogs (and humans) have a limited short-term memory capacity. On average, humans can store about seven things in their short-term memory at once, so we can assume this is similar in dogs. When we train dogs, we want to utilise as much of that capacity as possible in order to accelerate the learning process. However, if we use aversive methods, fear of punishment will take up a large percentage of the short term memory, therefore reducing a dogs' capacity to learn.
- Ultimately reinforcement will not be needed every time – Traditional trainers often have the argument that if you use treats or rewards, the dog will then expect this every time. However, this is not the case. Once a new behaviour has been learned you can gradually reduce the rewards given, so the dog is only sometimes rewarded for doing the right thing. This is called a **variable reinforcement schedule**, and it actually strengthens learning. However, for punishment to work, it has to be given every time the dog displays the unwanted behaviour.
- It allows owners to build a better relationship with their dog – If you are only ever perceived as a bringer of good things by your dog it will greatly strengthen your relationship. Dogs don't have

the capacity to understand if they are being told off "for their own good" in the same way that humans do, so it risks your dog becoming fearful of you. A positive relationship with your dog means they will be less fearful when you introduce them to novel situations because they will not be expecting you to bring a negative experience.

- It is much easier to reinforce the right thing than punish the wrong thing – When training a dog to do something new we generally have one goal which we would like our dog to achieve, and that one behaviour can be reinforced. Whereas there are an infinite number of things that the dog could potentially do wrong. Therefore, if we use punishment it can take hours to narrow it down until the dog does what you want, whereas positive reinforcement clearly communicates tot the dog what is the right thing to do.

- It is the only way to truly train calmness – Other forceful methods can train a "freeze", but not calm behaviour that is vital to a dog's wellbeing.

SHAPING

One method many trainers use is called "shaping". This means teaching a behaviour by reinforcing small steps towards the desired outcome, this is known as "successive approximations". For example, if you are teaching a dog to have a bath you might begin by rewarding her for stepping into the bath, then for having one paw showered, then the next paw showered, and eventually her whole body, leaving trickier areas like the head and tail until last. One analogy often used is to consider training like a ladder, and each new step is like climbing another rung of the ladder towards the end goal. This is a great training tool which we can use to incrementally teach complex behaviours. This is a really useful training tool, referenced several times throughout the book.

WHAT IS POSITIVE REINFORCEMENT?

Although it may seem obvious, what is and isn't positive reinforcement can actually be quite complicated. Positive reinforcement means adding something good to reinforce a desired behaviour. In instrumental learning, there four ways to change behaviour. All of them work and are covered here to help build your understanding of learning, but as responsible owners it is our job to make the both ethical and practical decision to stick to a positive reinforcement based approach.

Positive Reinforcement (R+) Adding something rewarding to reinforce a desired behaviour.	Positive Punishment (P+) Adding something aversive to punish an unwanted behaviour.
Negative Reinforcement (R-) Taking away something aversive to reinforce a desired behaviour.	Negative Punishment (P-) Taking away something rewarding to punish and unwanted behaviour.

Below are examples of each:

- **Positive Reinforcement:** Giving the dog a tasty reward when she settles calmly on her bed.
- **Positive Punishment:** Kicking the dog if she jumps up at the dinner table.
- **Negative Reinforcement:** Pulling on a dog's neck with a slip lead until she walks nicely.
- **Negative Punishment:** Putting the dog in a crate if they are getting too excited – taking away their freedom.

This only works if the reinforcement or the punishment is of value to the dog. Not many dogs will work for just praise, as this is not in itself valuable to the dog. Similarly, not all dogs will worry about a loud "NO" from their owners, hence why some owners then

Sometimes finding a stick or jumping in a pond are far more reinforcing than food.

resort to physically punishing the dog with a slap or a kick. Yet, for some dogs, being shouted at can be a petrifying experience. Being able to avoid these kinds of methods is another reason why positive reinforcement based training is a much kinder approach.

One common point of confusion is that the difference between positive and negative reinforcement can be a thin line. This is because negative reinforcement can take subtle forms. For example, some trainers recommend waiting until the dog is really hungry before commencing a training session. This is in fact negative reinforcement, as you are reinforcing the dog by taking away something bad. While this may seem like a good way to improve the dog's motivation, it can often lead to the dog becoming frustrated, and distracted by the feeling of hunger, and therefore less able to learn.

REINFORCEMENT SCHEDULES

One common argument people use against positive reinforcement training is that they do not want to have to use treats every time their dog does the right thing. However, the good news is you don't have to use treats every time.

In dog training, there are two main reinforcement schedules that we use in day to day life. These include **continuous reinforcement schedules** and **variable reinforcement schedules.** A continuous reinforcement schedule is when you reinforce the desired behaviour every time it happens. This is best used for teaching a new behaviour as it helps the dog pinpoint exactly what you want her to do.

Once a behaviour is learnt, you can move on to a variable reinforcement schedule. This is when you only reinforce the desired behaviour some of the time; meaning it is not the end of the world if you do not have treats to hand. The benefit of a variable schedule is that there is an element of chance as to whether there will be a reward, which actually helps to strengthen the dog's learning.

Moving on to this type of reinforcement schedule has to be done gradually. Begin by just missing the occasional reward. Then gradually reduce the frequency of reinforcement given to dog for performing the desired behaviour. If the dog struggles with this, the behaviour may not be securely learnt enough to move on to a variable reinforcement schedule, so there is no harm in returning to a continuous schedule until the behaviour is perfected.

ANYTHING CAN BE REINFORCING

Although treats are probably the most easy and convenient way to provide reinforcement for your dog, they are by no means the only way. Anything that your dog enjoys and finds rewarding can be a reinforcement. For example, a game of chase can be very rewarding for some dogs, or maybe playing with a favourite toy. The important thing to remember is that dogs live in the present, so need to be reinforced as immediately after the desired behaviour occurs, otherwise they will not make the connection that performing that behaviour leads to a reward.

CHOICES

Having freedom of choice is vital to the welfare of animals. Research has shown, just having choices, even if they are not acted upon, reduces stress. As owners, we control so much of our dogs' lives: when they eat, when they go to the toilet, when they go for a walk, when they see friends and whether a room is light or dark just to name a few. Now of course, many of these decisions are in the interest of a dog's safety, dogs can't just be sent off to walk themselves when they feel like it. However, there are some small changes we can implement that will help give dogs a greater sense of control over their own lives. Some ideas might be:

- A selection of different sleeping locations. Try to have at least a couple of dog beds for your dog to choose from, in different rooms. If you allow your dog on the bed and sofas, that's even better as it gives them another place to choose from, and also

Exploring on a country walk is a great way to exercise choice allows them to decide on whether they want to be with you or not, which is another important choice.

- When you take your dog on a walk, it is okay to listen if they seem to show a preference for a particular track. If it makes no difference to you, and is not dangerous, it might be nice to let your dog explore the alternative route she has shown a preference towards.
- Have several different dog toys that your dog can choose from. Try to find ones with different shapes, sizes and textures. This will also be beneficial for destructive dogs because if you reinforce your dog for playing with her toys, perhaps with a gentle game of tug, it will help teach the dog what is appropriate to play with and what is not.

SOCIALISATION

Socialisation is a really important part of dog ownership. It refers to introducing dogs (generally puppies) to a wide range of other dogs, people, animals and environments so they are confident in those situations later in life. This allows dogs to be better adapted to the human world they live in and better able to cope with potential stressors. There are many useful "socialisation checklists" online which can give you ideas of things it may be useful to make sure your dog is comfortable around.

However, socialisation needs to be handled carefully. Dogs should only ever be introduced to new things gradually, ensuring they do not display any fear. For example, if you want to introduce your dog to people wearing sunglasses, you may begin by leaving a pair of sunglasses around the house, or even a few different pairs. Then put the sunglasses on yourself, allowing your dog to see you wearing them. Then (assuming your dog is already socialised to a variety of people), have a friend or relative put on some sunglasses for your dog to observe.

Similarly, if you want to introduce your dog to new people. Do not simply have people come up and stroke your dog as this may be too much at once and make your dog fearful. Gradually introduce the smells, sights and sounds of people in a methodical way. The idea of **shaping** is really important here. You could begin by leaving some clothing of people unknown to your dog around your house. This will give your dog the opportunity to familiarise herself with the new person's scent. You could then use tools like the radio and the tv to introduce her to the sounds of different voices. To get the dog used to the sight of people, one idea may be a bench near a park where she can watch people go by, and even be given some treats as they do, as this will help her associate new people with good things.

Socialisation is a tricky concept, and for some people the best idea may be to find a positive reinforcement based dog trainer to support with this.

CRATE TRAINING

There is a big movement in the dog industry towards the use of crates. While these can be great tools for managing dogs, they should only be used with extreme caution. It should not be forgotten, that crates are essentially just cages designed to contain the animal, so understandably a dog, especially a puppy newly taken from her mum, is unlikely to feel at ease when put inside a crate. If you are concerned for your dog's safety, one better option may be to "dog-proof" a room in your house, which the dog can stay in when left alone rather than confining her to a crate. Not only is this is the best way to put your own mind at ease that the dog cannot harm herself, but also ensures that your dog still retains the important feeling of safety vital to their wellbeing. If you do choose to use a crate the dog should never be left in there for extended periods of time.

Situations when crates can be very useful is on car journeys, and if the dog is injured so needs to be confined for safety. For these situations it will be a great help if the dog is crate trained. The easiest way to do this is to begin before the crate becomes a necessity, so the dog is never locked in the crate before she is ready.

To begin crate training your dog, set up the crate in a nice area in the home (even if you ultimately plan to use it for car journeys),

Dogs sleeping in crates are much less likely to get adequate REM sleep.

put some comfortable, familiar bedding inside and leave the door permanently open. If the dog goes in by herself, reward her for doing so, and continue doing this whenever you see her using the crate. If she needs some more persuasion, you could hide some strong-smelling treats in there, and then reward her further when she goes in to find them. Once she is in the crate, practice sitting, and lying down, rewarding her for remaining calm inside the crate.

Once you have reached this step, you can begin introducing the door. Begin by closing the door for around a second, offering a reward, and then opening the door again. From there gradually build up the time that the door is closed. For example, one minute, two minutes, three minutes, five minutes, seven minutes, ten minutes. As the dog becomes more comfortable with being locked in the crate for a period of time, begin leaving the room, again just for a second, and then gradually build this up.

It is important to remember different dogs have different limits of how long they can cope with being inside a crate. Think about humans on plane journeys, some people don't mind long twelve-hour flights, however some people are terrified of just stepping into the confined space. Like humans, every dog is different, and when we ask our dogs to do challenging things, like spending time in a crate, we must stick to their terms and be aware of what they can cope with.

CAPTURING

One good training approach to use when working on new behaviours is 'capturing'. This means waiting for a desired behaviour to take place naturally, and then reinforcing it. So, in this case, waiting until the dog naturally chooses to settle down in her crate, then as she does this offer a high value reward. Repeat this process whenever you see the dog go to her crate.

Chapter 2 – Eating and Drinking

Eating and drinking is fundamental to survival, and therefore very important to dogs. It is important to remember that a dog's natural eating and drinking experience is very unlike how we feed our domestic dog. We expect them to eat out of a bowl, often alone, some dogs are given the same food every day and pet food looks completely different to what foods a dog would encounter naturally. However, we can take steps to make it feel a less alien experience.

EATING

- Feed your dog raw bones and chews – There are many advantages to this that greatly outweigh their unpleasant look. Firstly, they are great for your dog's mental health, chewing on a bone triggers a positive dopamine release that will improve their mental wellbeing. They are a great calming activity for energetic dogs that are easily over excited by walks and fast games such as fetch. They are also good for your dog's teeth, potentially saving you from costly vet bills in the future.
- Offer a variety of different foods and flavours – Most commercial dog foods nowadays come with lots of different flavours so take advantage of this and give your dog a selection. Eating should be a form of enrichment to dogs in the same way having a variety of different foods and meals is to us.
- Surprises – Dogs are also built to scavenge, so little surprises now and then can be great. Think how nice it is finding £10 on the street. Perhaps if you are cooking something and your dog is sitting down nicely, (providing the food is safe for dogs) you could offer her some.
- Temperature – Dogs naturally prefer warm food, most likely an evolutionary trait as this would suggest it is fresh. To mimic this, we can occasionally offer something freshly cooked to our dog or add a bit of boiling water to their wet food (although

make sure you give it time to cool). This again helps create a sense of variety vital to a dog's wellbeing.

THE CONTRA-FREELOADING CONCEPT

One popular idea in the dog industry at the moment is the contra-freeloading concept. This is the idea that animals prefer working for their food. It has been shown that animals generally will choose to earn food instead of being given food in a bowl. Many people have now adapted this into their dog training by using some of their dog's daily food intake as training rewards or creating puzzle games for their dog to earn their food. This is a great way to enrich your dog's life and avoid them becoming overweight.

However, if you do choose this approach, it is important that dogs still have normal meals as well, because having to work for all of their food is likely to cause frustration. Which completely defeats the object of providing this sort of enrichment. Imagine arriving at a restaurant starving and having to complete a crossword before being allowed your food. Puzzles and games like this need to be provided in addition to normal meals rather than as a substitute.

DRINKING

- Availability – It is important to ensure dogs always remain hydrated and have water available around their environment. It can be good where possible to have more than one location for this, especially in multiple dog households as it will ensure there is no contention over the water bowl.
- Flowing Water – Some dogs prefer flowing water, as this is more likely to be fresh. Some dogs can often be seen dipping their paw in the water to make it move. One option is to purchase a commercial dog water fountain designed for dogs with a preference for flowing water.

THE HYPOGLYCAEMIC EFFECT

When a dog has not had regular enough meals, glucose levels will drop below normal. This is called hypoglycaemia. Research has shown that hypoglycaemia reduces both humans' and dogs' ability to "gloss over" potentially provocative situations that otherwise they may be able to cope with. For example, this may be an unknown dog coming too close; whilst a dog may normally be able to cope with this, she may growl or snarl at the approaching dog if suffering from hypoglycaemia.

To counter this, it is always best to offer dogs at least two meals a day, to help maintain blood sugar levels. It is also important to avoid taking your dog out just before a meal, as this is when she will be least able to cope. Ideally, wait for around an hour after a meal, as this will give time for the food to take effect.

RESOURCE GUARDING

Food is a very valuable resource to any animal, and dogs are no exception. Dogs have evolved to be protective of food as it is fundamental to their survival. Therefore, we sometimes see resource guarding around food with our domestic dogs. Resource guarding is when a dog becomes aggressive or defensive behaviour to ensure others do attempt to steal the valued resource. It is important to understand that this is a natural behaviour, and not abnormal. If you are concerned a problem is developing, the best thing to do is to contact a qualified canine behaviourist for help.

As owners, we can also take steps to prevent the issue. The most important thing to do is always leave the dog alone when she is eating, so she is not concerned you will take her food away. Some traditional trainers advise taking the dog's bowl away and putting it back as a preventative measure. However, unfortunately this has the opposite effect because it teaches the dog that humans take away food and therefore can worsen the issue. Most dogs, if pushed hard enough will eventually become annoyed if their food is taken away repeatedly. Whereas, if we never take their food away, they are much more likely to be accepting if a young child or a visitor goes and disturbs them by mistake.

If you have a multi-dog household, ensure the dogs all have their own space when they are eating, and both are fed the same so there is no food envy. If you give one dog a special bone or

Being protective of resources is something dogs have evolved to do.

chew, ensure the other dog or dogs are offered one as well. This will help reduce any tensions over food between the multiple dogs.

MISUNDERSTANDINGS AROUND DOMINANCE

Resource guarding as described above is often confused with "dominant behaviour". Many traditional trainers and training books are based on an idea that dogs are trying to dominate their owners, and therefore it is important for the owners to show them they are "pack leader". This theory is based on an entirely flawed understanding of how dogs and wolf packs operate and can have a significant impact on a dog's welfare.

Dominant and submissive behaviours in wolves and dogs are extremely complex and could be the topic of a whole other book. However, the simple message is that pack structure is a social behaviour that only arises in extreme conditions in wolves where there is a shortage of resources. These conditions are unlikely to arise in a household environment where resources tend to be plentiful. Furthermore, dogs are completely aware that humans are not dogs, and do not treat us as such, so it is pointless for us to go around trying to act like the "alpha dog".

So, if a trainer stops the dog from walking out the door in front of him, or shouts at the dog for jumping up, the dog will not be linking this with any sort of household hierarchy. She will simply be confused and fearful of her trainer.

Body care is important to both dogs' physical and mental health. It is important they have well-groomed and kept coats and are able to go to the toilet when necessary. This section covers some basic husbandry training to help manage your dog's body care needs around the home.

TOILETING

Toileting is admittedly not the best part of dog ownership. But it is very important that dogs are given the opportunity to go to the toilet regularly and it is good for them to know where is and isn't an appropriate place to go. It is important to consider that, in most cases, dogs completely rely on us as humans to be able to be let out to go to the toilet. Cats have litter trays or go outside; horses go whenever they want and even smaller pets like rabbits or hamsters have completely free choice. Naturally, dogs would be able to go to the toilet almost whenever they wanted, so adapting to human life can sometimes be harder for some dogs. To help alleviate some of this stress it is important to give your dog regular opportunities to go out to toilet and not wait until they are desperate to go.

One of the most common difficulties, especially with puppies, is holding it in overnight. One way to help dogs manage through the night is with an understanding of the gastrocolic reflex. This means the act of eating stimulates movement in the gastrointestinal tract, hence why we often need to use the toilet after eating. We can apply this to dogs, by feeding them their dinner, not to long before bed, and then giving them the opportunity to go to the toilet around ten minutes later. This will give them the best set up for comfortably managing through the night and reduce the risk of accidents.

We can also teach our dogs where is and isn't an appropriate place to go, through simple training. When you think your dog may need to the toilets, lead them over to the desired toileting area. When your dog uses this area, offer them a reward, but ensuring it is not done in such a way it disturbs them while going as this can have the adverse effect. You can use this method to teach your dog to go to the toilet in very specific areas, which can be very useful if your garden is mainly patio.

If you are really struggling to get your dog to use a particular area, one option is to set up the place you want your dog to go by either placing some of your dog's faeces in the area or enlisting the help of another dog to do so. This will make the area look and smell like a toilet place which may then encourage your dog to use it.

It is really important not to punish your dog for having an accident indoors. This is because dogs do not discriminate between right and wrong, they just see what is safe and what is dangerous. So, telling her off for toileting in the wrong place will not teach the dog that going indoors is wrong, instead the dog is much more likely to learn that going to the toilet in front of her owner is dangerous. This will have a counterproductive effect, as it may stop the dog going to the toilet in front of you, which makes indoor accidents harder to find, and outdoor toileting much less likely to happen as you will be present.

BRUSHING

Some dogs naturally love being brushed, which is great because it makes being brushed a reward in itself. If this is the case, you could even begin to time brushing to be a reward after a good training session. However, for some even the sight of the brush is enough to send them running and hiding.

If your dog hates being groomed, the first step should be to buy a new brush. This is because dogs are very **context specific learners**, your dog is likely to remember the sight and the smell of the old brush and associate this with painful or scary experiences, and therefore may already be in a state of high arousal before the grooming even begins. Having a new brush will allow you to teach the dog that brushing equals a calm, reward based experience and establish a new, positive context around brushing. Find a new brush that is really soft and gentle on the dog's skin; do not worry if it is not effective for now. Taking the brush and a handful of treats, gently brush your dog, on her back, on a one brush equals one treat ratio.

Repeat this over a few days, gradually increasing the amount of brush strokes before you reinforce with a treat. Once your dog is entirely comfortable with this, move on to a more effective brush if necessary. If you do change brush, be prepared to go back to the one brush equals one treat ratio until your dog is more used to the new brush. Then continue to gradually increase the amount of brush strokes before reinforcing with a treat. If your dog walks away, just end the session there, and try again later.

TRIPS TO THE VETS

Vet trips are an inevitable part of a dog's life and can often be a source of stress for many dogs. This is fairly understandable as dogs' often have aversive experiences at the vets, such as injections, temperature checks or even operations, all of which can lead to the dog becoming very fearful of going. While these are often a necessity and unavoidable, there are still ways to reduce the stress of vet trips for both you and your dog.

- Avoid Waiting Rooms – Vet waiting rooms are often problematic places as they are often filled with very nervous animals about to see the vet. This means they are likely to be more reactive, and therefore scare your dog, adding to her stress. Fearful animals can release fear pheromones, which are likely to be picked up by your dog, again making the situation more stressful before it has even really begun.
- Practice at Home – Some of the most common veterinary procedures can easily be practiced as part of a fun training session at home, making them less daunting when they actually

take place. For example, for injections, even though you cannot practice injecting your dog at home, you can practice parting your dog's fur, then holding something similar in shape like a pen up to the back of their neck and offering a reward.

- Muzzle Training – It can be really valuable to muzzle train your dog, so then if your dog does need to wear a muzzle at the veterinary clinic, it will not seem a strange and unfamiliar experience. If you do muzzle train your dog, try to make sure she gets used to wearing the muzzle in places other than the vets, as otherwise she may start to associate wearing the muzzle with going to the vets. There is a section on how to muzzle train your dog later in the book.
- Bring a friend – If you have more than one dog, it can help to bring along both dogs together. Having company will bring an important sense of safety. Also, if you have an older dog, that does not mind the vets, a younger, more anxious dog may be able to learn from the older dog's calm response.
- Bank Positive Experiences – Many vets now allow people to bring their dogs into the vets at quiet times. Begin by calling ahead to check it is okay to visit, then take your dog along, and maybe practise some simple training or ask a staff member to give her a high value treat. This will help your dog build positive associations with the vets.
- Choose a good vet – More veterinary surgeries are beginning to offer 'low stress veterinary visits' for dogs and cats. Many vets and vet nurses are familiar with low stress handling practices and many veterinary surgeries are now set up in such a way to make the visit a minimal stress experience for their patients.
- Create a **discriminative stimulus** for calmness and use it for the vet visit – This is a slightly more complicated concept, however, has the potential to be very useful if applied correctly. A **discriminative stimulus** is something that tells an animal

something good is about to happen. For example, when we pick up the dog lead, dogs often become excited in the knowledge they are about to go for a walk. So, in the case of going to vets, you could use a special towel (or anything the dog will be able to recognise), that only comes out when you are about to sit down calmly with the dog and give her treats. Practice this regularly at home, until the dog knows that whenever the towel comes out, good things are going to happen. Then when you are at the vets, you can bring out the towel and start offering the dog treats, perhaps even ask if the vet would not mind offering your dog some nice food.

Many of these techniques can also be transferred across to trips to the groomers, or other places that may be a frightening experience for your dog.

This dog is practising a head rest which may be useful for future veterinary treatment.

Chapter 4 – Rest and Sleep

As humans, we know how difficult to function it is when we have not had enough sleep, and the same goes for dogs. Much like humans, a dog that has not slept well is more likely to be irritable and will struggle to learn. This chapter will help you gain an understanding of how dogs sleep, and how we can help give them the best conditions to gain an adequate amount of sleep.

The sleep patterns of dogs are not dissimilar to that of humans. They consist of both Slow Wave Sleep (SWS) and Rapid Eye Movement sleep (REM). Sleep cycles begin with SWS and then move onto REM sleep. In humans this happens over the course of the night. Unlike humans, dogs can split up their cycles into numerous bouts over the course of the twenty-four hour day. This is known as polyphasic sleeping.

During REM sleep, brain activity is high. It is likely that it is the time when the brain processes the experiences it has had throughout the day and consolidates important information. The electrical activity seen during REM sleep in dogs is similar to that in humans, leading many scientists to speculate that dogs have dreams like humans do. However, with current technology this is very difficult to prove.

DOGS' SLEEP NEEDS

Dogs need at least fourteen hours of sleep per day, and puppies need even more. We can help our dogs achieve this through a variety of means:

- Choices – Like humans, dogs have individual preferences, and as discussed earlier, choices have a big impact on a dog's feeling of safety and security, which is vital to sleep. Try to provide your dog with at least a couple of beds, in different locations which feel safe.

- Company – For dogs, sleeping is a social behaviour, so being expected to sleep alone may feel very unnatural and scary for them. Even for older dogs, social isolation can be a significant cause of stress. There is no harm caused by allowing your dog to sleep in your room or even on your bed, it actually has a positive impact on their welfare. If this is not possible, a second option may be to set up a dog gate between your bedroom and the landing, allowing your dog to see you when they are sleeping.
- Height – It is very common to see cats asleep in high places, because being higher up brings a sense of security, and to an extent, this applies to some dogs as well. You may notice your dog will choose to sleep on the sofa, or your bed, rather than their own, and this may be because they are raised. It may be beneficial to offer your dog a slightly raised bed, of which there are many different types available. The added benefit of this, is that it may even reduce the amount of dog hair on the rest of your furniture.
- Space – It is important that dogs are given adequate space when they are sleeping. If a dog is unable to lie flat and stretch out their paws, healthy REM sleep is much less likely to be achieved. When picking a bed for your dog, ensure it is large enough that it allows her to stretch out completely and that her whole body is well supported. This links back to another reason why crates can be such an issue for dogs as they often do not have adequate space to sleep.
- Freedom – This goes back to the idea of choices. If a dog is locked in a crate overnight, her feeling of safety will be severely compromised and therefore healthy sleep will be much harder to achieve. It is good to give your dog the freedom to move between at least one or two rooms so they can choose where they would like to sleep. You can also play around with

different variables to see which your dog prefers, such as temperature, lighting or even sounds.

CRYING IT OUT

One method commonly recommended with both puppies and children is self-soothing or letting them "cry it out". This is the idea that when you first have a new puppy (or child), you leave them on their own at night, and ignore any crying. Eventually they will stop crying as they will know it will not work.

This method is sometimes successful as eventually some puppies will stop crying and settle down quietly. However, this does not mean that the puppy is okay, it more likely means they are scared and have no way to ask for help, because crying was unsuccessful, dogs often give up. It is important to allow your puppy to be with you as much as possible to develop a secure attachment, which means they will be better adjusted for when you do have to leave them in the future.

Dogs often prefer sleeping on human beds or sofas as they provide additional height and space.

Motion and activity is essential to dogs' wellbeing. It is an important stress reliever and helps satisfy their physical needs for exercise as well as their emotional needs. Some of the activities described in this chapter can be quite exciting for some dogs, which is why it is important to always tie them in with calming games, described in the next chapter to ensure your dog does not become hyper-aroused.

WALKS

The easiest way to exercise a dog is taking her for a walk. They are great activities that most dogs love and provide a good way to meet other dogs and explore new places.

The best way to spread out walks is to keep them short and regular. When dogs go for a walk, they are experiencing a wealth of exciting smells, sights, sounds, textures and tastes. They may also see other

Harnesses are great tools for dog walks: giving the dog additional comfort and the owner greater control.

dogs, have moments of mild fear or anxiety and meet new people. While this is still great fun for them, it can also be overwhelming. This is why it is best to keep walks to around thirty minutes to an hour and try to mix up the different activities your dog may experience on the walk such as slow walking, fast running, sniffing and play.

It is also important to consider your dog's recent experiences. If your dog is in a state of excitement or has recently been frightened by something, they may well be in a state of "sensitisation". The adrenalin and other stress hormones in their system will lead to heightened reactions for around a few hours. This is something we might observe in ourselves after watching a horror movie or after a scary experience. If you think your dog may be too over-aroused for a walk, there are lots of other activities you could consider doing which are covered later in this chapter.

TRAINING A GOOD RECALL

When you let your dog off the lead, one of the most important things that you need to have in place to allow your dog to be safe is a good recall. Recall means a dog's level of ability to respond to their owner when called. A strong recall can take practice and work to establish, but it is an extremely valuable tool once properly in place.

The reason training recall can sometimes be tricky, is because we have to make coming back to us, seem more interesting than all the possible things the dog could experience off lead. One good way to overcome this, is through treats the dog considers really high value. This may be fresh meat like chicken or beef, or high-end shop bought treats often work well for this. It is often a case of experimenting to see what your dog gets the most excited about. Then, apply a specific cue for recall that your dog will only associate with those high value treats.

Training recall is not just something to work on when you are out on a walk, it can also be practised at home. In fact, home is a better place to begin practising initially, because it is an environment with less distractions. When you are around the house, simply reward your dog whenever you call her, and she comes to you. Another good place to practise is a fairly distraction free outdoor environment, such as a large enclosed garden. Practise the same thing, rewarding the dog whenever she comes after being called.

PLAY

Playing is a great enrichment activity in which you can spend time improving your bond with your dog. However, when we play it is good to focus on calm, mentally challenging games rather than physically challenging ones as this will help avoid over-arousal. Below are a few ideas of games you can play with your dog:

- Find it – Use a special toy that you only get out for this game. Teach your dog to pick up this toy when she sees it or when you say, "find it". Once your dog is familiar with how the game works, you can begin hiding the toy all over the room. You can then gradually build up to all over the house. Try to avoid making this game too difficult as this may lead to frustration.
- Catch – Catching is a really good alternative to fetch. Fetch involves fast running that mimics predatory behaviour and can result in the dog becoming adrenalised. Whereas catch relies far more on concentration from the dog to be able to correctly catch the item you have thrown for them, providing a good mix on physical and mental activity.

PROPRIOCEPTION GAMES

The following section contains some ideas for games that will help improve your dog's proprioception skills and provide fun alternatives to walks.

- Cones – These are a great, extremely versatile tool for games with dogs. You can set up cones in any order and teach your dog to walk around them, walk between them or some people can even teach their dogs to stack them up!

- Hurdles – This is an easy game you can begin teaching your dog indoors. You can buy specialist equipment or can use something as simple as an old wrapping paper tube. Begin by placing the hurdle on the floor and rewarding your dog for jumping over it, then once she is familiar with this slowly raise the height of the tube just by lifting it slightly by hand. Gradually build up to the height you want.

- Tunnels – Tunnels are a great addition to a proprioception area for your dog. Have the tunnel set up, and let the dog explore it at her own speed, do not push her in against her will. Instead if she is cautious perhaps throw a couple of treats inside it as a lure. When the dog first goes through the tunnel reinforce this with a good reward. If your dog is nervous of this you could always try to **shape** the behaviour by practising with shorter tunnels first.

Different heights, surfaces, textures and smells are all great for dogs to explore.

- Climbing – Providing ramps and low bridges for dogs to walk across provide a nice opportunity to hone your dog's sense of balance. This is where the target stick (explained on the next page) can be really useful to teach your dog to walk up and down the ramp, still remembering to reinforce this afterwards.

TARGETING

One technique that may be extremely useful to some of the following games is called targeting. This is when we hold out a marker that the dog will walk towards and follow. You can buy specialised target sticks, or make your own using things like fly swatters, wooden spoons or anything with a similar shape.

To teach this, begin by holding out your target stick close to the dog's face, and if she naturally goes and investigates, and taps it with her nose, reinforce this. Continue this for a few sessions, then gradually build up the distance between the dog and the target stick. Finally, introduce the concept of a moving target stick, and just reward the dog for following it.

BOREDOM OR STRESS?

One common diagnosis I often hear for stressed dogs is that "they are bored and need more exercise". The result being the dog gets tired out, meaning she cannot display her unwanted stress behaviours simply because of exhaustion. However, this does not address the root of the problem. For example, if the dog is anxious about being left alone, being tired out may stop the dog chewing up the house and destroying things because she is so tired, however she will still be just as anxious about being left alone.

If your dog is chronically stressed, just having more exercise is unlikely to be an adequate solution, going out more could even make things worse. It is best to contact a qualified canine behaviourist to get advice and help on how best to resolve the problem.

Chapter 6 – Exploration

When you take your dog for a walk in a new place, you may notice that they want to spend half their time sniffing the new environment. While to us humans this may seem pointless, it is important to remember that smell is the dog's primary sense, so to them it is a hugely important way to explore their environment. What may just look like a lamp post to us, actually carries a wealth of information about other dogs which have been there, when they were there, whether they are male or female and much more. This chapter discusses a number of ways that we can meet our dogs' need for exploration both inside and outside their home environment.

SCENT WORK

There are lots of ways to create great scent experiences for your dogs. Also commonly known as "sniffaris". Below are a few ideas, however I would also recommend coming up with some of your own as there is a world of possibilities.

- Scent Boxes – This is a great simple activity that can also be a great alternative for a walk on a rainy day. For this, you will need to collect lots of interesting and smelly things when out on a walk. This can include sticks, dead leaves, pine cones, long grass or hay. You can also top this up with things like screwed up bits of paper or old toilet roll tubes. Once you have gathered your materials, mix them all together in an old cardboard box, throw in a few treats for your dog to forage and then present this to your dog, giving them plenty of time to fully explore the box and its contents.
- Scent Cloths – For this, you can take a clean cloth, and rub it over an object such as an item of clothing, or another dog's house that your dog has never smelt before and then take the

cloth back and present it to your dog. This is also a good way to gradually introduce your dog to a new dog or human friend.

- Scent Trails – This is a really good activity for dogs, that can also be a great way to showcase the power of their noses. Fill up an old water bottle and mix it with a smell that your dog has shown an interest in in the past. Some ideas may be basil, mint, honey or ginger. Once the smell has had time to diffuse in the water, gently pour out the water in a trail around your garden and then present this to your dog.

- Let them sniff – Some people may tell you it's wrong to let your dog sniff, but this is not true. In fact, as this chapter discusses, sniffing is a natural behaviour for dogs and important to their welfare, as it has been shown to help increase dogs' optimism. Sniffing is a great way to enhance a dog's experience on a walk and provide them with mental as well as physical exercise.

Long grasses provide excellent sniffing opportunities.

PUZZLE GAMES

- Puzzle toys – These are great tools to help provide short, calming mental enrichment activities for your dog. There are many available now in pet shops and online. They are designed so your dog has to complete an activity like pressing a lever or lifting a lid in order to access the treat inside.

Leaves can be a good place to hide treats.

- Scavenging Games – Dogs have evolved as scavengers as well as hunters; something they often too keenly demonstrate as we see our food swiped in front of our eyes! One great game to harness this trait is to hide treats around your house for your dog to find.
- Scatter feeding – This is a really easy activity to do with your dog. As the name suggests, just scatter some foods or treats on the floor for your dog to find.
- Snuffle mats – One popular product now widely available commercially are snuffle mats. These are great tools which allow you to hide food in for your dog to forage.

AVOID MAKING THINGS TOO DIFFICULT

It is easy to assume, that just because a dog completed an activity quickly, it was not difficult enough. This is not the case, even just twenty seconds of nose work can be a really fun activity to a dog. If we begin making things too tricky in order to keep the dog amused for longer, this can often lead to frustration. This can result in the dog becoming over-aroused and more easily agitated, which defeats the purpose of a calming enrichment activity.

TOYS

Having a selection of dog toys is a great way to provide a fun activity for your dog, while also redirecting any unwanted chewing or destruction. Whenever your dog picks up one of her toys, engage in some play with her, this will help reinforce your dog for playing with appropriate items.

When picking out toys for your dog there are a few things to consider:

- Texture – Try to get toys with a variety of different textures for your dog to choose from. This will provide a range of different sensory experiences for your dog when investigating her toys.
- Shape and Size – A choice of different shapes and sizes can also be beneficial. Dogs are individuals and have different preferences. Some dogs may prefer large toys to drag around, whereas some may prefer smaller ones they can pick up and throw. This is also dependent on the size of the dog; a tiny dog might struggle to cope with too bigger a toy.
- Squeakers – Lots of dog toys contain squeakers, which can be fun activities for some dogs. However, these are not appropriate for all dogs, as the squeaker is designed to simulate hunting and lead to hyperactive behaviour.
- Alternate – Once you have gathered quite a few toys for your dog, one option is to begin alternating what is available. For example, if you have ten toys, you may only ever have five left out for the dog to play with. This helps keep the dog interested in her toys because things will always be kept novel and interesting.

Chapter 7 – Territorialism

This is actually a fairly easy need to meet. Just by living in a home with you, a dog's need for a home space will be met. The dogs' need for territory is one possible explanation for some undesired behaviours such as scent spraying and territorial aggression. Despite these behaviours often being considered a nuisance, they are actually very natural behaviours for a dog to display. We more often see territorial issues such as these arise in multi-dog households. This chapter explores a few ways you can help multiple dogs feel more secure in a limited or shared space.

RESOURCE GUARDING

To understand resource guarding, it is good to take an evolutionary perspective. Resources such as food or mates are often essential to survival, so if there are minimal resources available dogs will often compete over them. However, if resources are plentiful, dogs will generally be happy to share (while this is usually the case, some dogs do guard resources to an extreme level; if you encounter this it is important to seek professional help).

To help set up your home to avoid conflict, resource availability is an important consideration:

- Food – Try to avoid feeding the dogs next to each other as this may encourage stealing, try to feed them at opposite ends of the room, or if you are really concerned one dog will still try and steal, they can be fed in separate rooms. When possible, it can also help to feed the same food to each dog as this will discourage any stealing and potential conflicts.
- Sleeping Places – Ensure there are at least as many sleeping places in the house as there are dogs. Having lots of desirable places to sleep reduces the chance of any contention being caused over the one good sleeping spot.

- Water – While it is less common for dogs to resource guard water, it is still useful to have multiple water bowls around the house to avoid any issues arising around a singular bowl.

For this method to be effective all of these things need to be in different spaces. For example, if you have five beds in one corner of the room, it may just be perceived as one big bed, so resource issues are more likely to arise as one dog could potentially guard all five. However, if there are multiple beds distributed over a number

Space sharing indicates a good relationship.

of rooms, no dog can guard them all at once.

NAME RECOGNITION

In a multiple dog household, it is really useful for each dog to individually recognise the sound of their own names. Luckily, this is not an especially complicated behaviour to teach. It will, however, require you spending some time with the dogs individually.

Once the dog is ready and attentive, say the dog's name, and then when she looks at you, reward this with a treat. You do not need to reward any specific behaviour other than engagement with you at this point. When your dog has mastered this, practice it in as many different contexts and locations as possible, this will help the dog learn to respond to her name in a variety of circumstances.

TRAINING SETTLE SPACES

If you have a multiple dog household it can be useful to have a way to easily separate the dogs. This can be a useful way to intervene before conflict arises, separate the dogs for feeding, or keep them apart if you need to groom or clean them.

How you choose to implement this is up to you. The dogs could be trained to go to separate corners of the room. One way to train this is using mats (one for each dog). Soft doormats, towels, blankets and dog beds all work well for this. It is easier to begin training this with one dog at a time, however, more experienced trainers may be able to work on more than one dog at a time.

Begin by laying the mat out and encouraging your dog to explore it. As you lay the mat out, deliver your chosen cue word, for example "settle" for the dog to settle on the mat. The second your dog places even one foot on the mat, reinforce this with a treat. Keep doing this until she has all four feet on the mat. At this point, any engagement with the mat should be rewarded.

Settle mats can also be really useful in multi-species households.

Once your dog has worked out that standing on the mat is a good thing to do, begin to raise the criteria. It may take a few sessions until your dog is ready for this. Only reinforce her for actually sitting on the mat. If your dog becomes frustrated or struggles with this, go back to reinforcing her just for being on the mat and try again at a later session. Continue working on this for a while with all the dogs separately, until they learn that "settle" means they should go to their individual mats. It is important each dog is only trained with their own mat, so they know which one they are expected to go to.

Then begin trying this with multiple dogs. The easiest way to do this is enlist the help of a family member or friend (you will need as many helpers as dogs). Give the settle cue and be ready standing by the first mat to reward the first dog, and have your helper standing by the second mat to reward the second dog. Eventually you can begin increasing the length of time before you reward your dogs for going to their mats. Do this gradually, building up a few seconds at a time, until your dog will stay there for a reasonable length of time waiting to be rewarded. This will allow you to call out the settle cue, and then individually go around and reward all the dogs.

This is a fairly complicated training concept, so if you plan to implement it, it may be useful to look over Chapter 9 (Training to Reduce Your Stress) first or enlist the help of a qualified behaviourist.

Dogs have evolved as very social animals. The formation of packs allows for co-operative hunting, increased safety, and more animals to help rear new pups. Furthermore, play between dogs is a great way to facilitate bonding, relieve stress, and teach younger dogs how to interact socially. This is especially important if your dog does not have another companion of the same species at home as social isolation can be a big cause of stress for dogs. However, setting up a social interaction for your dog can seem daunting for fear that the dogs may not like each other, may play too roughly, or even start fighting. This chapter covers some ways to set up positive social interactions between dogs.

PREPARING FOR SUCCESS

When setting up dog to dog introductions, preparation is really important. It allows us to control the situation, so it has the best chance of success and ensures that things do not get out of hand. A few considerations are outlined below:

- Scent swapping – One option is to give your dogs the opportunity to smell each other before meeting (this is briefly discussed in chapter 6). Take a clean cloth and rub it against the dog you want to introduce, then give this cloth to your dog so she can get used to the smell of the new dog. Do the same for the other dog, giving them a cloth that smells of your dog to investigate.
- Location – The location you choose to introduce two dogs can make a big difference. Where possible try to aim for somewhere away from either dog's home to ensure there are no territorial issues. This is not to say other dogs can never come to your home, but it is better for your dog to be familiar and comfortable with them beforehand. It should also be

somewhere that both dogs are comfortable. If a dog is in a strange new place, she is more likely to react fearfully to meeting a new dog. An enclosed field that both dogs are familiar with can work well.

- Off lead – If it is safe to do so, off lead introductions give dogs a much better chance of success, as they feel less vulnerable when their movement is not restricted. If you are worried from a safety perspective, you may consider attaching long lines to the dogs so they can easily be separated if necessary.

WHAT IS PLAY?

When watching dogs interact, it can sometimes be hard to tell if you are seeing play or aggressive behaviour. Play can involve lots of fast movement, growling, barking, mouthing or chasing so it can sometimes be very hard to tell between play fighting and the real thing. To identify which is which, there are key signals to look out for:

- Body Language – Look for bouncy, inefficient movements. Dogs that are playing may also incorporate signals such as play bows and wide "grinning" mouths.

Two dogs enjoying a game with a ball.

- Changing roles and activities – Dogs that are playing will regularly change activities, for example they may go from mouthing to chasing to rolling. Similarly, dogs that are playing will often reverse roles, so if they are playing chase, you might observe them regularly change who is the chaser and who is being chased.
- Self-handicapping – Properly socialised bigger dogs will generally not use their full strength when playing with little dogs, similarly faster dogs may limit their speed if they are playing chase with dogs slower than they are. Self-handicapping is a great ability dogs have to make play safe and fun for all participants.

Watching videos online can be a great way to practice spotting signs of appropriate dog to dog play.

IS IT DEFINITELY PLAY?

Even with these clues to look out for it can sometimes be hard to tell whether a dog is really enjoying a play session and wants it to continue. One way to check this is to remove the more boisterous and over-exuberant dog from the situation by either calling her away or luring her with treats. Once this is done, see how the other dog reacts. If they come straight back over, looking for more play, you know that they were definitely enjoying the game. However, if they do not, let both the dogs have a break from each other to calm down.

NOT ALL DOGS ARE COMFORTABLE IN SOCIAL SITUATIONS

It is easy to assume that all dogs love playing together, however this is not always the case. Some dogs may not have so well developed social skills; they may have one or two close friends but in general may not really be that interested in playing with other dogs.

If this is the case with your dog, do not worry. There is nothing wrong with being less social, simply respect your dog's wishes and focus on more human based enrichment activities. It is important not to force unwanted social experiences on your dog because this risks making your dog perceive the experiences as aversive, meaning she may become even less tolerant of social interactions with other dogs in the future.

Similarly, if two dogs do not make friends, that does not necessarily mean your dog does not like other dogs, it just means it may not have got on with that particular individual. We do not expect humans to get on with everyone, nor should we expect the same of dogs. If this happens, try finding your dog some different friends that she may get on better with.

Chapter 9 – Training to Reduce your Stress

This chapter outlines some important training tools that you can use to enhance your own training ability, making it a fun and low stress experience for both you and your dog.

CLASSICAL (OR PAVLOVIAN) CONDITIONING

This is not so much a training tool but is an important concept that will allow you to better understand many of the following techniques. Classical conditioning is when something that is originally of no significance is paired with something that is naturally significant to the animal. Naturally significant refers to something that naturally triggers a response from the animal, for example, food, playing or danger.

For example, a common instance of classical conditioning in humans is in the case of alarm clocks. On its own, the sound of an alarm clock is neutral, it causes no emotional response. However, once we begin using an alarm clock to wake up to, an emotional response is eventually paired with the sound of the alarm. This is because we begin to associate the sound with a bad thing, in this case, having to get up. Some people even experience a feeling of panic if they hear the sound of their alarm clock during the day, reflecting the power of this kind of conditioning.

This is exactly the same in the dog world and explains a lot of our dog's fearful behaviours. If a dog goes to the vet, and gets an injection or a temperature check, that experience can be instantly associated with going to the vet, causing the dog to behave fearfully when she goes there again in the future. The dog could also associate the fear with the veterinarian themselves, and if she sees the vet when out on a walk, may suddenly behave fearfully with seemingly no explanation.

In these situations, where dogs present seemingly irrational fear, it is important to take them out of that situation as soon as possible, otherwise you risk creating a response called **flooding**.

Flooding is where something that is aversive and fear-provoking is continuously presented in a situation from which the animal cannot escape. This is a method occasionally used to help humans overcome irrational fears, so it easy to assume that it would work for animals too. However, this is not the case, and usually leads to the animal's fear rapidly escalating.

It is important to consider, that when an animal is frightened, its capacity to learn is greatly reduced. Imagine trying to learn algebra while being chased by an armed gunman; this is not unlike how it can feel for a dog being forced to face something that she is really frightened of. If a dog is scared of other dogs, having to go up close to other dogs may feel like life or death to the frightened dog and it can often lead to her fear escalating as a dog's ability to think and learn is impaired when she is fearful.

However, we can also use the classical conditioning process to our advantage in order to create positive associations in our dogs' brains. For example, in one of the classic experiments, Pavlov conditioned (taught) the dogs to associate the sound of a metronome with food. After several pairings, a positive association was created with the sound of the metronome. The dog's learnt that hearing the metronome meant good things were coming.

When a dog has previously formed a negative association with something, for example, reacting fearfully if someone grabs her paw, we can actually change that association with a tool called **counter-conditioning.** This means changing an animal's emotional response to something from a negative to a positive one. So, in this example, the trainer may begin by just lightly touching the dog's paw, then offering a reward, and gradually build up to touching the dog's whole paw. This process eventually teaches the dog that having her paws touched means good things.

CLICKER TRAINING

One of the best ways we can apply classical conditioning to dog training is through a concept called clicker training. This is the idea of using a sound or marker to show the dog she is doing the right thing. The sound most commonly used is a clicker. The dog is first taught that the sound of the clicker means a reward; in scientific terms the clicker is positively conditioned. Once the dog knows that as soon as she

Clicker training can really help dogs engage in a training session.

hears the sound of the clicker she will be rewarded, it can be used in more advanced training. You can usually tell when a dog understands what the clicker means because as soon as they hear the sound, they will start looking for their treat.

Once the dog knows the meaning of the clicker, you can begin using it immediately before offering a food reward in training sessions. What the clicker really helps with is pinpointing the exact moment that the animal is doing the right thing. This buys you marginally more time to deliver the reinforcer.

TIMING

In any sort of training, whether you are using a clicker or not, timing of the reinforcement is crucial. Dogs live in the present and focus on the direct consequences of their actions. You cannot reward a dog for a lying down once she has got up again and started doing something else, because the dog associates the reinforcement with the last thing that happened. When we want to reinforce a behaviour, the sooner after the desired behaviour the reinforcement is delivered the quicker the behaviour will be learnt. When training a dog, it can be helpful to use a treat bag or have a handful of treats ready to go to allow for faster delivery.

Similarly, timing is also key to any punishment, and poor timing is often the reason punishment is unsuccessful in resolving undesired behaviours. For example, if the dog chews up the couch while the owner is at work, the owner may come home and punish the dog. However, this may be hours after the dog actually chews up the couch, so the dog has no idea what is making her owner mad. If the dog chewing the couch is a common occurrence, it is easy to misinterpret the "guilty look" dogs often display after events like this. However, in cases like this, the "guilty look" is likely to be caused the dog's generalised fear of being told off when the owner gets home, and this fear is often the cause of these destructive behaviours in the first place. This is why the easiest solution is to avoid punishment altogether.

DELIVERY

The way the treat is delivered to the dog also makes a big difference. Ideally, once the dog does the right thing, you want them to receive the treat as soon and as easily as possible. Methods such as throwing the treat to the dog or dropping the treat on the ground run the risk of decreasing the dog's rate of learning. This is because, in these methods, the dog is reinforced for good catching of the treat or good foraging for the treat, which can sometimes distract from the original behaviour being taught. This is why it is useful, especially when teaching new behaviours, to try to stick to just quickly presenting the treat to your dog on an open hand.

Lying down can be a really useful cue to teach your dog.

USING CUES

Cues are the verbal or visual information we give our dog that tells them what we want them to do. Some examples might be words, hand signals or whistles. For some behaviours, we do not need to include cues, for example, with crate training, the presence of the crate acts of as a cue to tell the dog good things will happen when they get in the crate. However, for some behaviours such as recall, lying down or sitting, cues are commonly used.

Before an animal can learn a cue, they first need to learn the desired behaviour. For example, if I was teaching a dog to lie down, I would begin by using the method of capturing (discussed in Chapter 4) to reinforce the dog for lying down. Once the dog knows that lying down is a desired behaviour, I will then add the cue. Here are two ways to do this:

- The easiest is to wait until you see the dog about to about to perform the behaviour naturally, and then give the cue and reward her for doing so. Eventually the dog will make the association that to earn the treat, they need to perform the behaviour when they hear those words.
- Another method is to teach the behaviour as before. Once the dog has been consistently reinforced for performing the desired behaviour, give the cue you want to use for that behaviour, and see what the dog does. There is a chance the dog will perform the behaviour, and if she does you can

reinforce this with a treat. If they do not, move onto doing something else that the dog will enjoy. Then simply try giving the cue again later.

CONSOLIDATING LEARNING

Learning generally is more efficient in a distraction free environment. This relates back to the fact short term memory has a limited capacity, so if dogs are taking in information about new environments and unusual surroundings, they will have less short term memory available to learn and consolidate new information. So, for dogs, it is often preferable to begin learning a new behaviour around the house, as it is a familiar environment so there will be less distractions.

The way to overcome is by giving them the opportunity to practice these behaviours in as many different settings and contexts as possible. If your dog is struggling to perform a previously learnt behaviour in a new context, do not worry, try to avoid becoming frustrated and just continue practising in a less provocative environment.

WHEN THINGS GO WRONG

If the dog makes a mistake during training, do not worry. Try to remember this is not the dog's fault, they just do not yet fully understand what is required of them. If this happens, all you need to do, is not reinforce the behaviour, just wait for a couple of seconds, and then either try something easier or try again. This is a really good technique for training new behaviours, as it provides the dog with really clear information of what will and will not earn the reinforcement, without the use of intimidation or fear, which would slow the learning process and may just make the dog want to do something else. If the dog is doing something you do not want them to do, for example chewing up furniture, ignoring will not work because the act of chewing is self-reinforcing. So, in these situations, we can

redirect the dog's behaviour either by encouraging them to come and play with toys or calling them over for a training session. Similarly, in these situations, punishment is rarely effective, as the dog will simply learn it is not safe to perform the behaviour around you, whereas with redirecting we are helping the dog build alternative strategies for use whenever.

Dog's cannot be stubborn, deliberately naughty or disrespectful, they just do not always know what you are asking of them.

If your dog is repeatedly struggling with a task, it may be that you need to break down the task into smaller steps to give your dog a better chance of success. This goes back to the idea of shaping. For example, if you are teaching your dog to lie down on her bed, you may need to go back to reinforcing your dog for just having one foot on her bed, or perhaps for standing on the bed before you expect her to lie down and stay there.

This chapter only covers training basics. I have tried to keep it fairly simple and it should be enough for simple behaviours such as sit and lie down. If you want to find some more complex training tools that can help you teach your dog more advanced things, see the recommended reading at the end of this book. However, I aim for the information provided here to give you a strong foundation of training understanding that will help you move onto more complex training theory if you choose to.

FOOD GUARDING DOGS

Some dogs have problems with resource guarding around food, and if this is the case with your dog then food rewards may not be an appropriate training tool. It is likely your dog will benefit from seeing a behaviour consultant, who will be able to help you find other ways to work with your dog and help resolve some of the issues your dog may be facing.

This chapter explores some training you can put in place to help reduce your dog's stress.

LEARNING TO RELAX

One behaviour, easy to overlook when thinking about dog training, is relaxing. Settling down and relaxing is really important to dog welfare and encouraging dogs to be more settled around the home. While this sounds complicated, it is actually a fairly easy behaviour to teach. Whenever you see your dog naturally settle around the home, pick up some treats, and calmly present the dog with a reward for doing so. Continue rewarding this behaviour with regular treats for a couple of minutes, or until the dog decides to get up and leave. A good method to enhance this process is to have a high value treat used specifically for relaxation. This means, whenever the dog smells the treat, she will know that it is time to settle down and relax. You can also introduce a special blanket or mat for this, that only comes out when you want your dog to settle down.

Beds are a great place to reinforce calmness.

ACCEPTING TOUCH

It is really useful for dogs to be able to tolerate touch in all sorts of places. This is useful for so many different scenarios including: bathing/cleaning your dog, medical examinations, and in case strangers approach your dog and touch her without gaining your permission. As a side note, people really should not be going up and touching dogs without checking with the owner first, however some people are less informed on dog etiquette, so it does happen.

Dogs can be taught to accept touch through application of the classical conditioning process. For example, if a dog does not like having her tail touched, you may begin by gently touching her somewhere she is comfortable such as her back of shoulder area and rewarding this. Then after a few sessions, gradually move onto the base of your dog's tail, all the time clicking and pairing with a treat. This will start to change the dog's emotional response to being touched to a positive one. They will learn that touch equals treats. You can then gradually build up the touch to a greater level. Remembering to stop if your dog walks away or starts seeming uncomfortable. It is important to make sure dogs still have a sense of choice as to when this session ends.

MUZZLE TRAINING

Muzzle training can be very valuable to dogs. One reason for this is that they may be required for a veterinary examination. Being taught that the muzzle is not a bad thing beforehand will help reduce stress on the day of the vet trip. It will allow you to muzzle the dog happily before even leaving for the vets, without the stress of it being applied by a stranger in unfamiliar circumstances. Training a dog to tolerate a muzzle can initially seem like a fairly tricky task, because it is not a very natural feeling for a dog to have a strange device placed over her snout. However, with some work dogs can be taught to happily accept muzzles being taken on and off.

For successful muzzle training, the choice of muzzle is an important factor. Basket muzzles are good options as they fully cover the snout and allow the dog to be fed treats when it is worn. Begin by luring the dog into the muzzle by placing treats or paste inside the it. Then move onto holding a treat on the other side of the muzzle so the dog has to reach in to earn the treat. Eventually you will reach the point when you no longer need the lure, and you can wait for the dog to place her snout inside the muzzle, and then reinforce this afterwards. This means that the dog has learnt that placing her snout in the muzzle will earn reinforcement.

CAR JOURNEYS

Car journeys can be a big source of stress for some dogs. This can be for a variety of reasons – they may not enjoy the feeling of a moving vehicle; they may feel trapped in the small space or they may associate the car with a bad experience like going to the vet. Whatever the reason, there are steps you can take to help make car journeys a more pleasant experience for both you and your dog.

The first step is to counter-condition the dog to the car itself. Spend a few sessions reinforcing the dog just for being near the car, and then inside the car, while it is stationary, with the doors open. Keep these sessions really short at first, and then you can gradually build up the length. Once the dog seems comfortable and practised at this, begin closing the door for short periods of time, building this up gradually as before. To ensure you are not **flooding** the dog, keep the lead slack at all times, so she has the choice to walk away and end the session if she chooses.

Once you have practised spending time inside the car while it is stationary, and the dog is comfortable with this, you can begin introducing very short journeys. It is best if you can tie this in with a positive experience that you know your dog will enjoy such as driving to the local park or a friend's house. This will begin to teach the dog that car journeys can mean good things will happen.

Try to make sure the dog has more positive car experiences than bad ones. If a dog is not a fan of the vet, and the only car journey she has is to the vet then chances are she will associate car journeys with trips to the vet.

COMFORTING FEARFUL DOGS

One common piece of advice given is not to comfort fearful dogs, as this may reinforce their fearful response. However, this is not the case. We have all experienced being scared, and I know, if I am scared and someone is nice to me and offers some reassurance, I might actually feel a bit better; the same applies to dogs. Similarly, if a dog is scared and everyone responds by ignoring her, she may begin to feel even more fearful as the people she is close to and trusts are suddenly acting strangely.

Chapter 11 – Management

When caring for a dog, management is an important concept. Management means controlling the circumstances so things cannot go wrong. This is something we commonly do with young children when we keep sharp objects out of reach, or do not leave them unattended for long periods of time. A similar concept can be applied to dog care, allowing us to prevent incidents before they even happen.

Management strategies such as these will not solve the underlying problem, they simply prevent the problem from arising or worsening. For some people this is an acceptable solution. However, when trying to change behaviour, they are best used in conjunction with either a behaviourist or trainer to help resolve the underlying issues.

PREVENTING PROBLEMS INSIDE THE HOME

This section covers a couple of questions to consider when looking after your dog around the home:

- What is accessible to the dog? – If you leave lots of expensive, breakable items in reach of the dog, there is a risk that they might get broken, or your dog may even injure herself with them. Try to keep these out of your dog's reach where possible, especially when she is unattended. Providing dog toys is also important as it provides your dog with an appropriate outlet for playing behaviours.
- How does your dog react to noises? – Some dogs do not cope well with the sounds of passers-by, or things happening outside. One option is to have a radio which can be switched on when your dog is home alone, as it will block out the potentially stressful sounds of the outside world.
- How long can your dog cope with being left? – If you have to leave your dog at home, it is really important to know the length of time they are able to cope with, and not exceed this.

Some dogs will be fine for a number of hours, whereas some dogs struggle with more than an hour. It can be good to give your dog things to do while you are away such as puzzles or chews. However, this only will help relieve boredom, if your dog becomes anxious after a certain amount of time do not let it get to that point as it may lead to the dog becoming even more anxious about being left. When leaving dogs home alone it is also really important to consider their social needs. They have evolved to be social animals so social isolation can be a significant cause of stress for some dogs. Ideally it is better to leave dogs in pairs or more as this will give them a far better sense of safety.

WALKING A REACTIVE DOG

Going out can be stressful if your dog is fearful of other dogs or humans, however, while you are working through issues like these, there a few things you can do to keep walks an enjoyable, low stress experience.

- Time things carefully – Throughout the day, there are times that will generally be busier than others. This will differ depending on your local area, so being aware of busy times, like when school ends or when lots of people are on lunch break can be beneficial. Another option some owners choose is to walk their dogs late at night, which greatly reduces the chance of running into any other people or dogs.
- "Anxious Dog" leads and harnesses – Nowadays, as people and businesses are gaining a greater understanding of dog behaviour, there are a lot more products available for anxious dogs. Dog owners may consider investing in a lead or a harness that says "nervous" or "shy" to deter strangers from approaching. One even better option is a yellow vest for the owner to wear, as this is more visible and will prevent people

from staring at the dog, which could make her feel uncomfortable.

- Choose a good location – While local parks are sometimes more convenient, they will generally busier more often through the day. Wooded areas with lots of different routes can be good options as they are usually less busy, and easily allow you to change direction if you do see someone. Another really good option is to consider hiring an enclosed field. More people are beginning to offer out enclosed spaces for people with anxious dogs to hire to practise going out in a safe predictable environment.

If your dog is experiencing behavioural difficulties the best thing to do is seek professional help. Identifying behavioural problems early can make a big difference to the animal's prognosis, so if you are in any doubt, err on the side of caution and seek a professional opinion. Below are a a list of professionals you can contact:

YOUR VETERINARIAN

The first step, for any behavioural issues or sudden changes in behaviour should be to speak to your veterinarian. This allows you to rule out any medical issues or changes that may be affecting your dog's behaviour. If the issue is not medical, they may also be able to suggest a local behaviour consultant.

DOG BEHAVIOUR CONSULTANTS

Dog behaviour consultants are specialists in resolving behavioural issues in dogs. They will be able to help you put together management strategies and a behaviour modification plan for your dog. It is important to find a consultant that is part of a recognised organisation that uses up to date methods. These include the International Association of Animal Behaviour Consultants (IAABC), the Animal Behaviour and Training Council (ABTC), the Association for the Study of Animal Behaviour (ASAB), the Pet Professional Guild (PPG) or the Natural Animal Centre .

DOG TRAINERS

Dog trainers can also be a good source of help with teaching your dog new things, and tackling training related problems such as pulling or poor recall. However it is important to find a dog trainer that only uses positive reinforcement exclusively. They may also be able to recommend a behaviour consultant if your dog is experiencing more complex issues.

VETERINARY BEHAVIOURISTS

Veterinary behaviourists are vets that have taken further training to become a behaviourist. This gives them a great overarching view when managing conditions that may have both medical and behavioural components. If your behaviourist or veterinarian is struggling to get to the bottom of a particular problem, a veterinary behaviourist is likely to be the next person they will refer you to.

USEFUL WEBSITE ADDRESSES

- Dog Dedication (my own website):

  www.dogdedication.org

- International Association of Animal Behaviour Consultants:

  https://iaabc.org/

- Animal Behaviour and Training Council:

  http://www.abtcouncil.org.uk/

- Association of Pet Behaviour Counsellors:

  https://www.apbc.org.uk/

- The Pet Professional Guild

  https://www.petprofessionalguild.com/

FURTHER READING AND REFERENCES

- Simpson. H (2008): *Teach Yourself Dog.* Natural Animal Centre Library Publication.

- Bradshaw. J (2012): *In Defence of Dogs.* Penguin Books, London

- Becker. M, Radosta. L, Sung. W, Becker. M (2018): *From Fearful to Fear Free.* Health Communications, Deerfield Beach.

- Pryor. K (1985): *Don't Shoot the Dog! The art of teaching and training.* Bantam Books, USA.

- Reid. P. J (1996): *Excel-erated Learning. Explaining how dogs learn and how best to teach them.* James and Kenneth Publishers, California.

- Coppinger. L, Coppinger. R (2001): *Dogs: A New Understanding of Canine Origin, Behaviour, and Evolution.* Scribner, New York

- Rugaas. T (2006): *Calming Signals*, Dogwise Publishing, Norway

- Abrantes. R (1997): *Dog Language: An Encyclopaedia of canine behaviour,* Wakan Tanka Publishers, USA

- Overall. K (2013): *Manual of Clinical Behavioural Medicine for Dogs and Cats,* Elsevier, USA

Index

Printed in Poland
by Amazon Fulfillment
Poland Sp. z o.o., Wrocław